"Luci Shaw's poems have always been we
so in anxious times. There is a substantial
in language, creation, people, habits. Her poems reveal a mind marked by
humor, curiosity, good nature, and, well, generosity.
Each poem in this new book is a short lesson in noticing the world attentively,
and a reminder to slow down and find the wonder, not just in the natural world,
but in the less lovely things that make up our ordinary lives and duties.
Time spent with Luci is time redeemed."

—**Mary Kenagy Mitchell**, Executive Editor, *Image*

———

"Ah, *The Generosity*! Such an apt title for anything having to do with Luci Shaw
and her vocation as a woman of letters, a woman of compassionate engagement
with persons, places, and things. A profound generosity of attention, of vision,
and of connection with other souls is what is most apparent in these epistles of
the heart. Most moving to me—one of her thousands of longtime fans—
is her candid appraisal of the human point of view, and her diligent
νῆψις, or watchfulness, assists our own seeing, our own slow trek
to what may yet await us, *after* the in-between."

—**Scott Cairns,** author of *Slow Pilgrim: The Collected Poems* and *Anaphora*

———

"A new book by Luci Shaw is a reason for rejoicing! She gives us a generous
collection of lyric poems, reminiscent of Dylan Thomas, with lines such as 'The
air is full of green pilgrims who / walk together in this God light.'"

—**Barbara Crooker**, author of *The Book of Kells* and *Some Glad Morning*

———

"These poems illuminate how in poetry, as in faith, 'ripeness is all.'
With Wordsworth, Luci is celebrated for being a gifted landscape poet,
rich in imagery, but animals too, great and small (beetles, cricket, voles, bears,
and whales) play a major role in her poetics of creation. God is likened to a great
bear who leaves paw tracks for us to follow.
In their deep faith and vibrant colors and designs, the poems in
The Generosity might be considered Luci's Book of Kells."

—**Philip C. Kolin,** author of *Reaching Forever: Poems* and Distinguished
Professor of English (Emeritus), University of Southern Mississippi

ALSO BY LUCI SHAW

Poetry

Listen to the Green (1973)
The Secret Trees (1976)
The Sighting (1981)
Postcard from the Shore (1985)
Polishing the Petoskey Stone (1980)
Horizons (with Timothy Botts, 1992)
Writing the River (1994)
The Angles of Light (2000)
The Green Earth (2002)
Water Lines (2003)
Accompanied by Angels (2006)
What the Light Was Like (2006)
Harvesting Fog (2010)
Scape (2013)
Sea Glass (2016)
Eye of the Beholder (2018)

For Children

The Genesis of It All (with Huai-Kuang Miao and Mary Lane, 2006)

With Madeleine L'Engle

WinterSong (1996)
Friends for the Journey (1997)
A Prayerbook for Spiritual Friends (1999)

Nonfiction Prose

God in the Dark (1989)
Life Path (1992)
Water My Soul (1997)
The Crime of Living Cautiously (2005)
Breath for the Bones (2007)
Adventure of Ascent (2014)
Thumbprint in the Clay (2016)

The Generosity

Poems

Luci Shaw

PARACLETE PRESS
BREWSTER, MASSACHUSETTS

For John, and John, and John

2020 First Printing

The Generosity: Poems

Copyright © 2020 by Luci Shaw

ISBN 978-1-64060-514-5

The Paraclete Press name and logo (dove on cross) are trademarks of Paraclete Press, Inc.

Library of Congress Cataloging-in-Publication Data
Names: Shaw, Luci, author.
Title: The generosity : poems / Luci Shaw.
Description: Brewster, Massachusetts : Paraclete Press, 2020. | Summary:
  "In their deep faith and vibrant colors and designs, the poems in
  Generosity might be considered Luci's Book of Kells"-- Provided by
  publisher.
Identifiers: LCCN 2020011849 (print) | LCCN 2020011850 (ebook) | ISBN
  9781640605145 (trade paperback) | ISBN 9781640605152 (epub) | ISBN
  9781640605169 (pdf)
Subjects: LCGFT: Poetry.
Classification: LCC PS3569.H384 G46 2020 (print) | LCC PS3569.H384
  (ebook) | DDC 811/.54--dc23
LC record available at https://lccn.loc.gov/2020011849
LC ebook record available at https://lccn.loc.gov/2020011850

10 9 8 7 6 5 4 3 2 1

Published by Paraclete Press
Brewster, Massachusetts
www.paracletepress.com

Digitally printed

Heaven deliver us, what's a poet?
Something that can't go to bed
without making a song about it.

—Dorothy L. Sayers

CONTENTS

—

INTRODUCTION

———

O ne Christmas my husband and I sent out an original Christmas card, as we have done for as many years as I can remember. Someone had posted on Facebook an image of an ancient, weathered stump, in a forest, from which a fresh green leaf had shot up, like a mixed metaphor. It reminded us both of an image the prophet Isaiah had presented in Isaiah 1:11: "*A shoot will come up from the stump of Jesse; from his roots a branch will bear fruit.*" (see "Prophecy," p. 109).

As usual, I wrote a poem about this happy surprise and John illustrated it. Often, I feel as old as the stump, and I'm as shocked as anyone that poems keep surfacing, arriving without strenuous labor on my part. I'm not claiming to be the fulfillment of an Old Testament prophecy, or that I'm that burgeoning shoot of green, simply that I'm attempting something improbable at the age of 91, and that I feel enlivened as fresh shoots of words jump off pages at me, demanding my attention (see "While Reading *The New Yorker*" p. 28). This is but one of many examples of the sort of thing that keeps happening, sometimes at inconvenient intersections in my life.

The title of this collection, *The Generosity*, is a reminder of the prodigal green that flourishes everywhere in nature, despite our human depredations. And of the generosity of the Creator who planned the green of the world in a regenerative process that replenishes itself in cycles of seed and sprout—I'm still thinking of my Christmas card image—and growth and leaf and flower and fruit. This generosity gives us the means to celebrate not only our bountiful natural world, but our humanity with possibilities for displaying love and sharing and forgiveness.

I seem to write no matter the prevailing conditions. The Spirit has me tethered. I write out of enthusiasm rather than discipline. A snowstorm. A bad cold. Visitors. Grocery shopping. Needing a nap. Driving in the country. Cooking dinner. Making our bed (or feeling the guilt of leaving it unmade). Immediacy is my mistress, so what I am doing at my age makes me seem like a rebellious teen let loose on the world. It's a bit of a stimulant in that I feel high when the words are charging into my mind, demanding entrance.

I began to write before I can remember. My parents read me good books, and language intoxicated me from the get-go. My dad loved to read aloud the skillful prose and poetry of the classics. This gave me a feel for how language works. This understanding was enhanced by my later studies in Latin and Greek, which allowed for a greater understanding of the derivation of words and their rich usage in English. Not a poet himself, my father read anthologies and could quote the best lines from Wordsworth or Coleridge. I began to put little bits of paper with writing on them into his pocket. He carried these handwritten small poems in his briefcase to show to friends. I wrote a poem about this (see "Family of Origin," p. 77). It got me started, and so far there seems to be no compelling reason to stop.

Many of the shards of verse in this collection are auto-biographical, distilled out of routine experience that somehow rounds a corner and wants its turn on the page, hoping to say something fresh, surprising. I cannot live day-to-day without some impromptu clue snaring me into a fresh rush of words. That's the fun part. The real discipline involves pruning, shaping, eliminating, emphasizing, following the track that invites me willingly to experiment. I write during sermons in church, on road trips. I try to take a nap and a phrase will barge into my tired head and need to be recorded in the little notebook that accompanies me like a pup on a leash. Next, of course, I transfer those seed ideas into my computer. Sometimes my fingers are feathers, stroking the keyboard softly until the stanzas are safely captured on the screen. Occasionally I feel like Dorothy Sayers, who commented, after completing a sonnet, "I feel like God on the Seventh Day!"

Here, then, is a collection bearing witness to this generative life I am grateful to have received. If generosity is the keynote of these poems, gratitude is the melody their making has brought my way. I pray that it might be so for you, reading this, as well.

THE NEED TO HOLD STILL

Some simple happening just
makes you want to be there, to
listen, becoming conscious of
what you see, and cannot see. Yet.
It may announce itself—a knock
on the door, a word familiar enough,
but wearing a different color.
Sometimes the thing knits itself
row on row, line on line,
like a word garment that fits
imperfectly, waiting for revision.

HOW?

How shall we sing the Lord's songs
in a strange land? The old rhythms,
the melodies of praise, strangle
in our throats and the words
fall to the ground like leaves in autumn.
The air thickens with suspicion and doubt
and who's to say, anymore, what
is true enough to last, to prevail?

Isolation feels like a punishment
for offenses we never performed.

Let us trust, now, the ground under
our feet—that which has proven steady
for generations. Look up. The heavens
are still there, unclouded, beatific.
We breathe, even though masks clothe
our faces. Prayer surrounds us, close
as our skin, weaving for us garments of
trust and solace. Even in our isolation
we are joined in love, never alone.

VIRUS

The absurdity of a world
on its knees, behind its doors,
whose fingers, even, may be traitors
and whose breath, created for living,
may breed death. Its instruction:
Split up. Stay apart. This is now
the ultimate act of friendship.

Like the moon of light at the bottom
of the well, hope shines small,
but if we stay, head over edge,
we may watch the deep water shimmer
with supple possibilities. At noon,
a pale sun shines, telling us
we may still live in the light.

A WILD EMBRACE

How creation dares us into
a wild embrace of what is
too beautiful to ignore. You open
your front door.
Breathe, and all the old dust and confusion
of your life falls behind you.
You are not to obsess about it,
no matter how it calls you.
Instead, bend and examine
closely how the grass has grown
an inch under last night's rain,
and the peony buds are swelling,
the tips of pink petals already
bursting free like prisoners
wrongly convicted and now
released. There is such generosity
out there, reaching towards you
with hands open, claiming you,
a created being issuing
from the open mouth of God.

WAVE ACTION

I long for a charged encounter
with whatever is so lovely
I find myself transformed.

Listen. Have you heard
the sound of a wave
retreating down the angled stretch
of just-swept sand, edged
with foam that shrinks
with the sound of lace?
Does it tell of regret at
having failed to conquer
the great beach? Or is it
gathering itself for the next
onslaught?

It is a sound I sometimes hear
internally—a vital endeavor fading,
but leaving a kind of silver
anticipation.

BIRDS

I note the trajectory of swallows,
their little knife wings cutting the sky
horizontally, at great speed.
They forage in flight, exuberant,
building mud nests under
the overhang of cliffs, one beakful at
a time. The way some poems grow
incrementally, cell by cell, lyric
nestlings in the clay cups of words.

As the minor blood vessels that
irrigate the brain narrow, shrink with age,
will my thoughts diminish, grow
insignificant? Will the lines of poems
shrivel, abbreviated, mere ideas
in flight, then lost to sight?
Will they discover value among
the vast flocks of other words?

THE PLANE TREES
—by the River Seine

So, you decide *this* is worth
writing about, or painting—
the shapes of the branches on
the trees, how the afternoon sun
gleams on the variegated trunks,
how their reflections echo in the river.

You cannot change the image;
it has been there for centuries.
All you can do is move your own
body, shifting the angle here and there,
back and forth, so that you
see the thing differently,
until you find a satisfaction.

Is this how we solve
the enigmas of living? Things are
what they are and God is
who God is, unchangeable.
To satisfy our souls it is we
who must move, or be moved,
within the contours of grace.
Until. Until a fresh composition
in space, where light will
beautify our faces enough to
rearrange us in a fresh, particular
space in the creation.

"EVERY CREATURE IS A WORD OF GOD"
—Meister Eckhart

Expectant, we process into
the pine forest with its architectural trees.
No candles, but between twigs
patches of Godlight fall
at our feet. In this arboreal cathedral
we are supplicants for grace, worshipers
of viridian words being
spoken into the air every hour
like music.

Silence like a stilled bell—
this is also a word.

Incense lifts
from pine needles underfoot.

And look there—an ant with his
thready waist, blessing God
that he is small and black and
has a crumb to carry.

Two squirrels, fleet as furred angels,
chase and chatter.

We listen for a bird choir, something
a cappella. But in a small pond's lap
a frog with gold eyes coughs twice
in praise of water threaded with reeds
gleaming like a sung psalm.

INCOMING TIDE

The words arrive like waves.
Before I get one written down
another, just as energetic,
foams into consciousness.

The poet must puzzle out
which to swim with, which
to let go.

The way we tread a fresh footpath
across the pebbled beach
out of a longing to reach the ocean.

The way love develops energy
as it peaks toward
the insanity of passion,

or a dozen iterations before
the finished painting. By beauty
we may not mean perfection.

NOTES ON A CLOUDY DAY

Mistress of the in-between,
the not-quite yet, I watch my shadow
lengthen, shrink and join
other apparitions shaped by light and
dapple, leaving flecks of history,
a tatter of clues to what
might have been.

Every sound—waves crashing,
the symphony, your lover's whisper—
relaxes into silence like
the wind that sends leaves
flying and then dies, leaving only
snarled impressions
of muddy shoe leather.

My heart, grown sober and ice-hard
from winter relationships, turns
soft with the image of a day
when we will all sing
cherry blossoms and mottles of
white clouds.

THE MORNING, WALKING

The beauty of the world is God's tender smile at us
coming through nature.
—SIMONE WEIL

It's as if Creation is listening, absorbed
in contemplation, just being there. Like me.
Landscape claims me as its inhabitant
where I am, wherever I am.

Here, on the trail, the air barely lifts a leaf
among the green curtains of trees
or stirs the mist laying its pale garment
over the hill, under the bridge, between the barns.
Even under fog Your day is radiant,
a common yet secretive beauty.
Distant traffic muted. Birds silent.
Be very quiet. Listen.

A frog barks once in the marsh reeds.

Beside the lane the sentinel grasses of autumn
hear Your unspoken edict, lifting
their pale gold seed heads along the verges,
speaking without words.

A bicycle passes. For the cyclist
the road is a river flowing under his pedals.
The easy sound of tires on gravel,
and then again the mercy of quiet.

I am not what I was an hour ago. Oh, Quietness,
Come home with me, show your green Self
through my window, away from the din of the world.
I claim You as I listen for You.

THE CREATION

Yesterday my mind
grew a kind of intricate
foliage, words gaining power
by accretion, images
stumbling over each other
in their desire to be
recognized, heard, spoken
as if they had been waiting
since the beginning.

I was God in Genesis.
I felt them forming—
the syllables arriving in my mouth
like developing fruit,
pears, apricots.

Some slippery, like
skinned grapes, or fricatives,
stones rough enough to be
spitted out, leaving a hole at
the heart of the fruit.

I gather them,
let their juice fall
onto a page. It is like spreading
food on a table.

MOSS, ORCAS ISLAND

The jagged rocks along the shore's
       western margin wear, like patched
upholstery, the blotch and mottle

of lichen. And on the island's other
       edge, sheltered from rough winds,
blessed with rain, moss grows

its green sofa cushions on the rocks—
       six inches deep of brilliant fleece,
sponges absorbing light—a velvet green

that shines with a bright gold
       infused by the sun. The vivid color
enters the window of my mind like

a delicious feast for which no words
       do justice. I open the car door
and cross the road toward the sloping

rocks, to reach and feel and focus on
       this magic fabric (my camera will carry it
to lighten some dull day in my gray town).

This living green climbs silently the trunks of
        ancient oaks and hemlocks, creeping
along their knotted roots, the same moss tendrils

fine as baby hair, and sphagnum, whose
        slow velvet grows now in memory.
My mind speaks into it, verdant.

WHILE READING *THE NEW YORKER*

A word flies off the page
and through an open window in
my imagination, a bird
that got in and cannot leave,
batting wings against
my walls and bookcases, uttering
piteous vowels of sound.

Frenzied, she aims at the light.
It is window glass and it knocks her out.
Seconds later, and she has come to life
again, still frantic for exit.

I move away quietly, closing
the door of my mind behind me
to lessen the anxiety in the room,
leaving the window wide
open. Later, after she has
found her freedom
a winged presence remains
and a feather on the floor.

Next week, maybe other
words will fly in, and I'll welcome them
to make their nests and lay
their little literary eggs.

PILGRIM

Meaning is a landscape
of boulders.

There, ahead of you,
a thorny wilderness.

You cannot leap over it. You
must conquer it stone by stone.

To traverse it,
you must find sure footing

and fortitude
in uncertain weather,

your fear like metal
in your mouth.

And yes, it is possible
to walk the knife edge of longing,

a blade narrow
as the path to heaven.

WHITE SPACE

This page, and any page in
any book I read, is a pale
sky in which, centered, the text
kindles in my eye, leaping
into focus, telling me—this
is where the author's plot develops
next, and next, and next.

My husband's paintings,
framed in snowy oblong mattes,
draw our eyes' focus to what
once caught his artist's eye
and urged his squirrel hair
brush, loaded with pigment,
to limn a landscape.

Also, my notebook, its small
blank pages pure as a guilt-free
conscience, waits ready as
a fallow field, for plowing
with dark lines of verse that
stutter, scattering like
furrows on farmland.

GREEN, SPRINGING

Down the hill, over the river,
beside the dirt track I walk slowly
enough to stop, to listen for the pale
whisper of increment floating from
the tassels, the maiden buds,
the nascent leaves lifting their heads
—little green flames, more
chartreuse than emerald.

Now I hear it clearly. They are
telling their way into being
and calling us to join in.
The air is full of green pilgrims who
walk together in this God-light.

It is the best season. There is
such courage in bursting life.
And yes, I promise, it is possible—
to fulfill God's reason for thrusting us
into full leaf, rooted in our
unique, particular ground.

ENTHUSIASM

Rejoice! leaps from
the crocus up-thrusting
through scarves of old leaves.

From river edge, where ducklings
paddle in the fresh freedom
of water.

Joy frolics with the young deer
in the open meadow, flooded with sun.

Ardor shines in each
star of cold, fulfilling some purpose
appointed by heaven,
like a choir of little children
off-key, but undimmed.

The splash
a drop makes
in a pond.

The flame-leap on a single
just-lit candle.

HEARTWORK

My heart is a bird
perched on the upper
balcony of my mind.

My heart is a
baby *in utero*
engaged in private work.

My heart is a stone
until I turn it over and
find life teeming
underneath.

DOVE

Surely Noah's dove
had a husband.
Along with all the others,
we guess they'd
entered the ark, a couple.

So why not him?

Those were the days
of patriarchy.
Female that she was,
expected to do as
she was told, patiently
repeating her
reconnaissance over
the vast sheets of water.

Wives are such
hard workers—out and back,
out and back, an empty beak,
without complaining.

Until, success! That green
olive leaf! We hope she got
a pat on her little pigeon head
for her hard work.

And once more. And this time
freedom. No way would she
go back.

MORNING GLORY

Early, and my bones begin to
wake and lengthen, stretching
under the covers. The brain cells
come to attention also. At the window
I finger the pull and swish of cloth
as I take night's curtain in my hand
and assist in the welcome of
light, the way it glances
through glass. And out there,
off the pear tree branches
and their generosity, having received
coins of rain in the night
that are there for the taking
and spending.

I pause, considering
the latent life of twigs, ready,
like me, to open their curtains
of bark, speak the green language
of rising sap, translating it into
blossoms, the way I speak a poem
into air, a pause before
necessities—prayer, clothes, breakfast.

In this tender light I am assured
I can carry with me this day
an unclouded amazement at
being in the world, and of it.

THE MEANING OF GRASS
Your bones shall flourish like the grass.
—Isaiah 66:14

To write about the lives of grass
you might want to inhabit a meadow,
maybe lying down for an hour, nestling in,
close to the earth, like an animal,
the seed-heads tasseling above you
in an air that smells hot and ripe and
primitive. A cricket or two. Bees bumbling
on wild clover. A hawk in the blue dome
arching over you. You invite a green juice
to flow in your veins for an hour or so,
for the stems to acquaint themselves with
your alien body, to know that you, with
a body that aches, that loves, that will fade,
that urges you to ground yourself, this day,
which is unlike every other day in your
breathing life. You doze, wake with a start,
knowing that the prophet had it right.

DRIVING TO WILLAPA
May 2019

Through a landscape ravaged by clear-
cut, the bald hillsides are mottled
with a stubble of stumps, like old forest
memories, the land now and then redeemed
by the glint of inlets, estuaries cutting in
from the coast, waters with the bite of salt.
Further south and west the vast, level
reaches are punctuated by tufts and rafts
of marsh grass in mud that anchors also
the drowned-out gnarls of trees, roots
rotted by wet, silver ghosts, all their
green gone, sentries, place holders.

Yet how rich are the roadside verges
with news of spring's impossible greens,
the mosses, the fresh, plural grasses,
the little white umbrellas of cow parsley
under a blue sky! It is this verdure
that always brings us hope, its vegetable
ambition thrusts, rises, flourishes among
the slopes' gray ghosts. It will not be
held back. Nor will the waters in these
wetlands. With the out-going tides, rivulets
ribbon their way through the mud in
an endless tidal drag to join the sea,

obedient to the moon's pull, and later,
threading back in as the tide rises.
Nature will never be contained.

MEADOW

All thy works shall praise thee, O Lord.
—Psalm 145:10

With the still camera of memory
I take the breath of the meadow
—that meadow that yesterday lay
just beyond the split log fence—up
from my lungs and release it for you
to inhale, to seep into your body
entirely, to rouse you from your
gray-brown dreams, to color your brain
sky indigo and sun apricot.

Begin exactly where you are. Begin
to move with a river rhythm until
some gleam flows and flowers in you
that wasn't there before. Last month's yarrow
and cow parsley have given way to purple
fire-weed, that beautiful bane, and blue
chicory, with its cut-paper flowers, and yellow
pea flower, and snowbanks of white
daisies, each a season's celebration.
And now, all the grass-seed heads turn
torch in the day's late sun like you, alive
to embrace it and celebrate, to be your own
bright bloom in the fields of the Lord.

COW SOUNDS

Maybe the cattle will come
to the pond and drink tonight,
giving off gentle, bovine smells
and mooing at each other as
warm cream swells their udders.
In Switzerland, we listened also
for the language of the bells on
their necks, as the great, milky
brown beasts with soft eyes move
towards barn and milking shed.

I watch also for the burly words,
sounds that emit growls
or thunder, but settle, later,
into soft, as the evening rain starts
(an altogether agreeable event),
and with the soaker come
gentler lyrics that river their way
into our ears as if we are
catchment ponds being filled to
overflow. Do not doubt this
brimming of possibility.

PRESENCE

I long to write a poem
spare as a small, open window,
allowing in only enough air
to move the curtains briefly
(a hint speaks truer than a gust).
Maybe there'll be enough
salt in it to alert you to the ocean,
somewhere out there, beyond
the red cliffs. You may even hear
waves breaking on gravel—
that coarse sound. Or you may
sense it only by intuition, the way
you know, without seeing, that
someone you love is nearby.

THE "O" IN HOPE

Hope has this lovely vowel at its throat.
Think how we cry "Oh!" as the sun's circle
clears the ridge above us on the hill.
O is the shape of a mouth singing, and of
a cherry as it lends its sweetness
to the tongue. "Oh!" say the open eyes at
unexpected beauty and then, "Wow!"
O is endless as a wedding ring, a round
pool, the shape of a drop's widening on
the water's surface. O is the center of love,
and O was in the invention of the wheel.
It multiplies in the zoo, doubles in a door
that opens, grows in the heart of a green wood,
in the moon, and in the endless looping
circuit of the planets. Mood carries it,
and books and holy fools, cotton, a useful tool
and knitting wool. I love the doubled O
in good and cosmos, and how O revolves,
solves, is in itself complete, unbroken,
a circle enclosing us, holding us all together,
every thing both in center and circumference
zeroing in on the Omega that finds
its ultimate center in the name of God.

FREE RAINFALL

How extraordinary that air is so public
and rain is free,
and that every day God writes the world again
fresh from his fervent breath.

We are stirred by the word *renew*
like an air from the south after months
of gray cold. This educates us for
other kinds of change.

It's like a prayer we prayed
that got no answer but rain, then it
turned out we needed rain, so
we got our answer.

MIDNIGHT RAIN

Letting down from the water-laden sky
the little fists of rain drum on
the skylight above our bed, imparting
their version of the truth of heaven.

I know that too often the rain will
hold off, the grass darken and burn.
In summer even the flies grow listless.
And that, too, is a half-heaven gift
calling us to thankfulness when the heavy
clouds burst open over the fields, as a
fresh and fragrant cool sweeps in.
We open our windows. We breathe
the change that renews us.

How lucky that a poem can be
made of nothing much. That we don't need
to wait for the weather to shift, words
arriving from somewhere, spattering
like rain on a page.

LANGUAGE

How the fresh words,
the insignificant vowels, the jots
and tittles, walk themselves
across a blank page, stumbling
over fricatives and semicolons
but getting up, not wanting to stop
at the end of the line.
Adjectives crawl to me like
strangers in a strange land.
And then the wrong word, the one
chosen by accident, the one
I don't even particularly
like, turns the poem into
a fresh miracle on the page,
and later someone I haven't
met, who reads the words
I've submitted to his journal,
is struck dumb with delight,
asking for more and sending
a small check in the mail that is
just enough for a great
bottle of cabernet.

FIRST DRAFT

I felt I came alive today
in a sentence that wrote itself,
arriving from some cavern
of memory, showing itself in shards
of light and shadow.

I observed this with some
surprise, as if it had appeared
suddenly from around a corner
in an alley of forgetfulness.

I devour books to the point that
I feel infected with a literary
malady, skin turning paper white,
eyes blurring. My food begins
to taste of printer's ink. When I die
I hope to be in the middle of some
prosaic paragraph in *Elements of
Style* so that my final words reek of
refined scholarship and skill.

RHYTHMS

How our days open and close
like windows
so we are not weary of either
light or darkness as they achieve
the elegant balance
we have come to count on
the way we count on food
and drink and love.

We need this steadiness, this
faithfulness in realities we
have learned to welcome. Like rains
in a dry season. Like the way
every night we are content,
eager to creep
under the fringes of sleep.

MODALITY

Every sound, waves crashing,
the symphony, your lover's whisper,
relaxes into silence like
the mad wind that sends leaves
flying and then dies, leaving only
snarled impressions of purple,
and tattered fog. It's like
folding laundry and laying it
in the bedroom drawers.

BERCEUSE

Sleepless nights, in an effort at boredom
thick enough to be soporific I would
self-soothe with the monotony of alphabets—
the English, the French, the Greek—
mentally reciting them backwards and
forwards—my old head still fluent enough
with the letters. In the Greek I'd go from
Alpha to Omega and back, realizing
as I did that God is at both ends and
in every letter, every crevice in between,
pressing home to me a kind of literate
omnipresence and the conviction that
I cannot get lost in this infinity. And at last
the beatitude of sleep settles in.

UNABLE TO SEE FAR

Unable to see far, I write
what's near. How snow
responds to footprints and
the garden to a spade.
How my cat's small lion face
relaxes under my caress.
How words fall through me
like water, though some
thicken into thoughts
like scars. How the two chairs
on our deck, each a foot deep
in snow, face each other as if
conversing about the weather.
How, today, when I
complained of cold,
my husband covered me
with the old green blanket
and I napped and dreamed
of summer. How this afternoon
one robin, having arrived
early, sits now on the
power line, thinking to himself
this is not so smart.

DANDELION

As the days warm and lengthen, the grass
is getting happy almost overnight.
Under my window the first star of spring
opens its eye on the front lawn. Yellow
as butter, it is only one. But it is one,
and in the nature of things, and like
the multiple asterisks seeding the night sky,
it will flourish and take over every
grassy bank in town. I long to be prolific
as the dandelion, spinning pale parachutes
of words. Claiming new territory by
the power of fluff. The stars in their courses
have bloomed an unending glory
across the heavens, but here in my yard
a local constellation prepares to launch
multiple, short-lived, radiant coronas
to proclaim the new-sprung season.

LOWER CATARACT LAKE, COLORADO
—for James Scott Smith

Out from a grassy bank three mergansers
head over lake water patterned
with its own gray chevron waves.
Someone has taken their photograph and
shares it online—the weave of the ducks'
own transient V-shapes on the surface
behind them. How deftly the patterns
work together to leave a design
printed in the mind long after the ducks
have flown and the waters are stilled.

DRIVING TO WINTHROP

The landscape sings as it flashes
past your car. Lakes like mirrors.
You notice a seeping rock face from which
a thread of water falls, like a plume of
white hair down a crone's back.

You are ravenous, your eye never
weary of seeing—the vine maples
bleeding their ruddy flush beside
the highway, and in the benevolent sun,
the aspens flaunting their gold sequins.
Your camera not surfeited,
no matter how many, how often.

Near the summit the verges
are tricked out with dregs of snow,
mottled by melt.

Beyond, east of the Continental Divide,
the Methow runs glittering through
the little town and down the valley,
rivering over rocks and gravels, between
banks of willows. (You hear the sound still,
a liquid rippling in your inner ear.)
It sings its water songs to the bare

flanks of the hills, giants sleeping,
worn silky-brown by centuries,
arching their backs into the penetrable blue
where, up high, a plane leaks its
white contrail against the indigo sky.

DUSK

This night, just the sound of the word
spells for us the tender way darkness
is falling, gradually, but with intent.
We're camped, lakeside, evening covering us
with its mantle of calm, and a single,
sequin lightning bug shows up, then two.
Three, then the air is a glimmer of twinkling
lights—a whole constellation: "*There!*
There! And right *There!*" hovering over
our dying campfire, intimate and magical.

As the night deepens the sky comes close
and the lake mirrors such an array
of incandescence we can hardly breathe.
And now, in the twilight's sorcery, a loon
sings his silver sliver of descending sound
like a kind of primal ritual, telling the night
he is part of the magic, carrying
the light of those stars on his back.

STREAM OF CONSCIOUSNESS

A trip with rod and reel never sends you home
empty; no poem ends at the bottom of the page.

My own darting bait of a metaphor floats
through your watery surface—the quick membrane

of your eye—beyond the rounded bank
of your skull, and feels its way along

a million neurons, waving like water weeds,
to an untroubled pool where it rests, waiting,

a sliver in your slow flow. Without fail,
almost without volition, you will catch

your own golden carp on the silver hook
I am trailing through your cerebral current.

EVE

What was it like for her,
recovering from recent surgery,
to lie down on the red earth
next to the stranger from whom
she'd just been detached,
with whom she was lately an
integral body part, drawing in,
now, her first breaths of Eden air,
wild with the fragrance of fresh
flowers? Looking down at her lovely
nakedness, did she anticipate being
a mother, every one of us draining
out of her pale body? I ask her:
Did you dream, even for a moment,
that your blood could run rampant
in my bones? And do I have
your hair, your eyes, your hunger
for fresh, forbidden fruit?

RUMI'S REQUEST

When I threw away my old eyes,
grass grew from the sockets.
—RUMI

I begin to think of my ripening body as
a sack of fertilizer richer than compost or
plant food from Costco.

So, when it is time, bury me shallow,
my skull a bowl of bone with
eye sockets easily entered (into the space
once occupied by thought) by small,
damp organisms.
They will feed like kings.

Think what bone marrow will accomplish
as it leaks into the soil and nourishes
nematodes. Beetles will love me.
I'll be humus. Instead of weeds and
crabgrass, I will grow green grapes
and wheat. Jasmine will flourish above me,
sweet with the smell of my dying.

THE CONTINENT OF NIGHT

Yesterday the leaves fell, as they will,
and the air acquired distance and
a cold clarity that invited us to see higher,

telling us it is time to stop and look up,
to let the sky arrive, filtered only
through the dark webs of branches.

And later, the continent of night
with its celestial array came
so close we could hardly breathe.

DIURNAL

How the days open and close,
like windows,
so we grow weary of neither light
nor darkness
as they achieve their fine
balance. We have come to
count on this as we count on
food and drink and love.

The sun rises like a man
from his bed, getting to work
for us as we move through
the hours. If you have errands
to run, or wish simply to sit
and read, he is there for you.
And at day's end,
having earned his keep
and retired, you wish him
a good night's sleep.

And if you are out late,
walking, you will be grateful
if the moon-woman
paints the streets with
her pale pewter,

laying a silver garment over
roofs and chimneys,
and later, sending her hand
through your window
onto your pillow. Even if
you cannot sleep,
you give thanks.

THE WEIGHT OF AIR

The bird wears the sky on
her back, lightly, an extension of
an iridescent plumage.

Feel the sky. Wear heaven like
your halo. Doesn't your head
gleam with it, when happiness
happens, as if you were freed from
gravity into a delirious levity?

Sometime, enough of us should plan
to gather and form our own
luminous cloud.

SPECULATING

What we cannot see,
only imagine, hoping
our guess is true.

The ancient, secret roots
anchoring a Douglas Fir,
so patient, spreading in
the long dark.

Moles, also. And the vole
in his safe burrow, and
the secretive nests
of snakes.

We chip at the edge of
knowledge, excavate our own
hidden longings for
understanding.

WHAT MY BONES TELL ME

That they'd hope for a bit of credit
for shoring up this fleshy boat in which
the soul finds a way to swim the world.
For steadying this sack, this pouch
of blood and fortitude.

I cannot get away from me,
walking around with secrets
inside—my box of magic tricks—
airways that catch and release
breath, reaching the lungs purely,
without particulates. A tongue that
manages a thousand pleasures.
Eyes like moments of light.

I count on my nerves' reminders.
My hungers wear me like
a colored tent that God enters
at my invitation, and sometimes
without it, teaching my flesh
obeisance of spirit.

HER DEMENTIA

Is a jigsaw puzzle with
a missing piece—
blue sky with a hole
where the light leaks out,
taking the words
with it.

In the daily paper
a crossword, the clues
incoherent,
words that don't fit
the spaces, blanks
with no letters.

A railroad track,
the rails ending at
a cliff-edge. No
bridge in sight.

ON BEING TESTED

She leans forward, searching the doctor's
face for clues. She thought she'd aced
the baseline—*Count backwards by sevens*
five objects an apple a ladder a ball
a mirror an envelope what's the date today
fold this sheet of paper in half and drop it
on the floor—what do you think she is,
a first-grader?

There's an anxiety in the air.
How to anticipate what's next, and is there
a next and what does it look like and
how long?

The CT Scan of her brain has
shown its claws and waits.

Her daughters are with her. Together they
rummage for answers, for words to hold onto
on this shifting ground, for a measure of
calm, of acceptance. "What's next?"
she asks, listening for a voice of wisdom.

Before they leave the clinic the doctor lists
the meds and they inquire about side effects. It all
feels provisional. She longs to find sense
for this journey that doesn't yield to
sensible inquiry. She holds to the known
unknown. She's not alone.

TELLING THE DREAM

All night the mattress pressed up
under my bones, forcing its way
into my sleep like
the floor of a tent on gravel.

In the narrative of sleep the bed
grew to a beach on which
dreams flooded and overflowed and
broke and drained away,
leaving a muddied trace
of last night's color and calamity.

Morning, and in my attempt to
rehearse the vivid narrative
with you, my night companion—
the train travel that morphed into
a swimming pool, the lovely meteors—
the images break apart
as words get in the way of my telling.

How to hold on to them.
How to let them go.

MIDNIGHT

In bed, and a kind of loneliness
   settles.
I am wakeful, wondering.
    I reach out my hand from under
the sheet, and over the edge
   into the empty space beyond,
and feel for God's hand, his large
   callused palm, a shallow cave,
fingers curling their intimate way
   around mine. Not a word
spoken, but in the dark air a glow,
   like a night light near the door.

VOICE

The voice is a silken muscle.
It caresses the vowels like
rosary beads strung on consonants
until they become prayers offered
in thanks to the Word for language.

So, while I wait, listening for
husky syllables, sounds that emit
grumbles or thunder or waves breaking,
I like to settle into soft
as the rain starts, a gentler lyric
that rivers its way into our ears,
ponds brimming.

PLUNGE

It's what I long to do, abandon
caution and dive into the violent
blue at the heart of the wave,
swimming deep, leaving behind
the swirl of shore-sand and seaweed,
the coarse sting of brine in the mouth,

yet here I am at the edge, the sand
sucking at my feet just where the waves
leave the lace hem of ocean,
the foam imprint, the transient
signature of the Pacific.

The aroma of desire
as the tide goes out and fog rises.

THE RULES

How I am bound by time
and its unflinching hours!
How to be free of clocks,
calendars, binaries. Of
highways running both
ways, and the center line
that insists that we stay in
our own lane. Of the window
thermometer and its rising
red line that dictates what I
will wear today. How to
find a notebook with no rules,
with smooth blank pages
to write on, vertically or at
a slant depending on my mood
(even a tentative sketch of
a tree or a curious pebble).
To sleep until I feel like
waking, hours ahead of the
alarm, or later. To acknowledge
that light is both a particle
and a wave like me, when I'm
unsure exactly why I believe
what I believe. To be flexible
about what to make for

dinner, and relaxed enough not
to feel guilty if my husband
kindly suggests we go out. Or
write a poem with no discernible
rhyme-scheme that happily
meanders across the page.

FEW WORDS

To write with
restraint, with
few words,
is to give each
a great power
that stands
for itself on
the page—
this red bird,
that crescent moon.
Each sentinel
of meaning
pointing us
to what
it stands for.

WILD

On the door mat a tuft of
blue-gray feathers and, two days later,
a tissue of white bird-bones
fine as lace. And now our house cat,
intrepid hunter, whose feral blood
wakes at the sight of wings in flight,
sits there, purring velvet, licking
his paws and staring us down with
his bold green eyes.

FAMILY OF ORIGIN

Our parents keep circulating
in the rooms of our lives.
Mine are long gone, but if it would
satisfy them I would take my heart
out of its cage and gift-wrap it
for their anniversary.

I glimpse them often, Dad reading
a book over my shoulder,
now and again offering words
of advice that might have made
sense fifty years ago. The words
form clots in my memory, cells
bright as blood, a private language
unlike any other.

My mother demanded mountains
of me. I managed to supply foothills.
They were lovely foothills, but
failure would hang in the air. We still
seem to meet in the heart of an old
argument, words hanging unresolved,
glittering sparks in the dark air.

Sometimes, when I feel most wrong
about how to remember them, I am
most right, seeing them as they settled
into the grooves of my own memory.

I am my own narrative arc,
yet I arrange the candles and
flowers on my mantelpiece the way
my mother would have done it.

And for my father I still write
small poems, like the ones he
carried in his briefcase to
show his friends when
I was very young.

MIRROR IMAGE

I move from room to room. In every glass
my face looks back at me and asks,
How can you know a version of yourself,
see yourself true enough to trust you are
no lie, no sham, the same inside and out,
you being truly you for who you are?

I turn my head. From across the room
the window's lights and shadows
stroke my skin, shimmer my cheek,
redefine my features (familiar more to others
than to me, living behind them).

I cannot look at my bathroom mirror,
then look away and see myself from memory.
Nor can I trust my sideways profile
halving me in the glass, nor take
some camera's version of my face as truth.

Constrained by surfaces, my self
is flattened to a plane of cold silver, no hint
of my hidden interior. Distance is not
an answer. Further off, my reflection's merely
dimmed, unfocused and inferior.

The glass allows only a shallow deceit,
my countenance reversed,
turned wrong-side out. Thank God
he needs no lens to know the me
that's deeper than my face. Knowing that
I'm not gone when all the lights are out.

SOME MORNINGS

You just want to stand outside, quite
still, and breathe. And breathe,

and breathe again, the green
scent of grass after last night's raindrop
calls you to take notice:

Here, for instance—
under your feet, the shapeliness
of clover, that brave, small

interloper, an unabashed invader,
having introduced herself into
your manicured front lawn,

with her heart-shaped trinities
of leaves, pearled with the
aftermath of rain (the dew of

heaven). How can we not admire
her fortitude against the threats of
mower and weed-killer as she

informs us, with becoming modesty,
*I was called into being
by the grace of God?*

WATERWAYS

Afternoon, and I walk alert,
listening for what the river sings
between her banks and under bridges.

As she flows along the margins,
she kisses the green reeds and rushes,
the water voles, floats the small river birds,
rinses rubble riverside, cools a pair of
traveling feet, carves banks wherever
she takes a curve, opens a water path
for fish, and, come evening, voices
her luminous mysteries in mist.

From the bridge I glimpse
her silver flow below, the flotillas
of leaves and waterweeds drifting
with hints of rush and bubble,
of subdued riffles over gravel.
And after a storm, flushed and
swollen, I join her, as some torrent
within me channels its way
along the valley to the Sound.

BENEFITS

Tide's out. The morning's rain
has left its signature, a pattern like
small footprints on the beach sand.
Soon, now, the tide will turn and
wash them away. Whatever happens
there are consequences. Results.
Like the delicious astonishment we feel
when our strawberry plants burst
into white blooms that transform,
growing plump and red thanks to
all the compost dug in last fall.

Does my flourishing blue and
purple hydrangea feel blessed because
I'm ravished by her exuberance?
Is my daughter the better for
my fond thoughts of her? What imprint
may I leave on the garments I knit,
shawls and children's hats and
small blue sweaters that I pray
leave a trail of warm?

GROUND COVER

You've planned your garden, encouraging
order, with glowing contrasts that come
and go with the seasons. Then, summer
arrives, and rain falls, and with
the encroachment of green, orderly yards
turn rampant, boisterous, thanks to
fertilizer, probing deep, crazy for
moisture, enthusiastic about sunlight,
indomitable, determined as parents
for their children's success.

I'll not complain when the Vinca Minor,
starred all over with her vivid blue in spring,
untidily overflows her summer borders,
mounding, creeping across flagstones,
a declaration that it's utterly okay to be
profligate in the celebration of loveliness.

THE BIRDS

Twilight, and some birds find
a branch convenient for
night's rest. Others
fly the dusk, carrying
the light of their stars
on their backs.

Sometimes there's
lightning, like nerves
running through your arm.

The canyon wrens of Texas
spilling their downward cascade
of song, a kind of tonal
language for which
no translation is needed.

THEME AND VARIATIONS

The air, sharp, smart,
a knife in the nose.

Beyond the sliding glass
door, the deck. A cluster of
bird-foot signatures pattern
a lacework of fine prints
on the tissue of snow.

Above them the feeder, thick
with sunflower seeds, sways
as five assorted families flirt
and fly and fight for access—
grace notes perching on
a treble clef. Juncos, towhees,
a pirate jay, house finches,
their breast feathers flushed pink,
black-capped chickadees: all
the small, hot bodies
canceling cold.

SKY BLUE

April and a glistening world,
a map unfurled beneath
a duet of robins, circling—
blue sky high, green meadow low—
an ardent tango. Boy bird
giddy with love, flirts with girl,
flings himself in avian pursuit, now
watching her winging away, then
drawing her back again into
his own flight plan. And again.
Again. His desire dancing
higher, further. And again, until,
demure, she agrees he's
the one and, finally fervent,
joins him in the mating dance.

Next, we expect a nest of
sky blue eggs.

QUOTIDIAN

The sun runs
its golden feet
across the wheat.

Wind
shakes the field like
a bedsheet.

Night,
moonlight, and
silver, like a million
herrings swimming.

THE KNITTING

First, it's the yarn that beckons,
fleece buttery with lanolin from
the just-shorn sheep, a woolly proof
against wind and rain. Combed, carded,
spun, it becomes a skein of possibility.
For color, dunk it in a vegetable stew—
petals, leaves, bark, seeds—until
it rises from the vat like an animal,
and offers itself into your hands.

It was the habit of my New Zealand
aunt to gather damaged fleeces from
the local farmers' black sheep. Once,
she mailed across an ocean ten pounds of
dense yarn, spun on her wheel, for me
to knit into a suit. Later, I ripped it out,
re-purposed it, ample material for
sweaters, socks, caps. Like the way
we sometimes need to switch directions
in our lives, developing original patterns,
growing designs never seen before.

PARTURITION

Someone's brilliant novel
seduces me with its
riveting language.

Inside me, something like
bread dough rising.

Fragrant syllables
arrive on my tongue, ready
for the oven, swelling
to a narrative to be
baked and served.

Maybe it's not my belly speaking.
Maybe there's still a womb
down there under my ribs, and a
metaphorical infant growing
up to birth.

I close the book and its narrative,
turn to my journal, with time and
a mixing bowl ready to whip up
a fresh batch of verses.

PEACHES

Look, you can get them at the local
supermarket, lined up, appealingly
angled towards you in rows in a bin.
You pick one up—a global flush of
pink and gold, soft-felted in the hand.
And yes, it will do for today, shipped
from Chile out of season for your
enjoyment, but hard as a rock, bred
for shipment. But it takes you back
all those years to the humid August
week in Illinois, your third baby just
days old, and your spouse brings home
for your pleasure a bushel—*a bushel*—
of Redhavens from Michigan. Images
of orchards, boughs heavy with little
suns just waiting for our delight and
the tang of sweet juice on our tongues.

You know in an instant what to do.
Think *thrift* and avoid waste, mindful
of your New England mother-in-law.
So, you nurse the baby, roll up your
sleeves and get going, dipping each fruit
in boiling water so the skin slips
away, leaving the luscious orbs naked

as a baby's bottom. You split the flesh
from each stone, measure the sugar, fill
to an inch within the brim of each
Ball jar waiting in the canning kettle
on the stove, ignite the gas flame, set
the timer, and let the magic chemistry
begin. Later, you line up the cooled
jars on your basement shelves, row
on golden row, anticipating the glory,
the taste of summer next winter.

MULTIPLES

A generosity of wind
shakes a colloquy of color—
poppies across a field
like salt.

A community of
emerald moss. My feet
test the velvet.

And on the sidewalk concrete
like a map of stars,
a collect of black ants.

THE HOUSE INSECTS

So this morning, I'm thinking of our local
inhabitants, mostly the reprehensible closet moth
and her soft stumble into light, leaving evidence
eaten into the collar of my blue cashmere
sweater, but really, what else is there for
a moth to eat?

There's the fly with his burnt-amber eyes
housebound in winter, having fruitlessly explored
our windows for exit, now and then cleaning his
stained glass wings with twigs of legs. I wonder,
do they ever gnarl and forget to untangle?
Now he lies stilled, on his back, legs crossed
on his thorax, a dark blot on our green carpet.

My nemesis, the house spider, expert at
home invasion, denizen of dark corners,
spinning her soft silk like a Hallowe'en
witch, draping it behind the books on the shelf
where she thinks I'll not notice. Evenings,
she descends by fiber from the ceiling
onto my face, loving me enough to want
my company in the dark.

MORE

The pitcher cries for water to carry.
—MARGE PIERCY

A thin trickle, even a drip
may start a river.

The heart, falling short of love,
pleads, challenges
my capacity. Fill me so full
my surplus overflows,
makes a little lake
of spillage. Make it a river.
Send it, foaming, over the cliff-edge
into a profound pool. Keep it
drinkable, fresh, unlimited.

TODAY

Today I feel
a little fear,
small as a crumb,
moist as a tear.
The reason for it
is unclear.

Not sure if it has
simply come
from something that
will disappear.

A minor fear
is all I feel.
It has a sense of
something real,
but likely it
is no big deal.

RELINQUISHMENT

My cells are
floating off,
scattering,
shavings
from the tool
of the Spoon Carver,
furring the floor
like autumn's
oak leaves.

And today
the fine hairs
released from my cat's
dark coat
imprinted
my white
bedspread.

SCANT

Is there a balance
to be found
between profit and
loss? A reward
for endurance?

Make it personal;
may I feed on
scarcity the way
Jesus did
in the wild,
subsisting forty days on
stones, the scourge of
the Spirit, the predations
of the Accuser,
the intent of
the Father.

Can what is scant
and spare be wrung
out of dryness
to yield some nourishing
essence?

We've learned about
nutriments in bone-broth.
Bodies are one thing,
but even the soul
has a structure that pleads
for more than mere
survival.

We discover this
only *in extremis*,
waiting there, longing
to be fed.

THE CHILD

He was everyone's hero, my father
the missionary doctor.
In retirement, though never fully,
he wore tweed and smelled manly.

Sixty when I was born, his first child.
(My mother, forty-even, gave difficult birth
under a sheet. I was named Lucy
and meant to be the light of their lives.)

Most of what he told me was true,
at least for him, his mind always angled at God
in an ecstatic slant that was too steep for me.
So, true? Was Jesus coming to rapture us,
and when, and would it be very loud and
would it hurt, flying through the roof?

London, and thick fog. Out shopping at Harrod's,
me waiting in the car, my five-year-old heart
pounding with panic that they wouldn't
come back, and I'd be left.

At night I'd beetle my way into their bedroom
to listen for their breathing and know
I was not abandoned. Yet.

I worried that I hadn't said the words in the
right order or sincerely enough, about
asking Jesus into my heart. Jesus
seemed too big to get in, anyway, and he'd know about
my lies that put the blame for lying
on my little brother.

Growing up, I could give God only a teaspoonful
of myself. They told me he wanted
an overflow, a firehose worth. It leaks
more easily now, tracking its salt down
the wrinkles on my cheek.

DARK FRIDAY
—after viewing Tintoretto's Crucifixion

So many traditional images of
Christ, the Lord—painters,
sculptors, speculating from their own
harsh lives, at an eon's distance,
how incarnation spoke to them, not having
been there, maybe paying a model
to be Jesus, the centuries between
coming almost alive under their fingers.

There are those of us who wish we, too,
could have walked in his shadow,
sketched him—dusty feet, blessing
bread and fish, canceling a storm
at sea. How would we depict demons
being evicted, signs and sermons and
our own, unsuccessful efforts
to understand? Wanting, even, to
follow him in the dusty streets,
to hold his hand, unknowing in
the moment, how that hand and
its companion, and the feet, would be
split and splayed against the tree
planted, grown, planned, foretold,
ever since the first forest.
Was the bloodied wood itself blessed

by the plunging metal that
held together the whole crude, cruel
construct against gravity, suspended
between earth and heaven?

How may we imagine the dread
of noon darkness as the local,
holy curtain tore open
the implacable night, as hope
died and, heavy as millstones, our hearts
plunged? How, now, may we
celebrate the radiant emergence,
the disruption that transfixed
the faithful, so few hours away,
ahead? How would we paint and
recreate resurrection?

PSALMODY

Always new psalms wait
to be written.

David, sweet singer,
had a mere life span to pour out
the river of his complaints,
passions, praises.
His overflow used words
open as bowls, feeding them into
those passionate couplets—with a
twist of direction that pauses,
midway, reflects on a metaphor—
the shadowy valley, skies full
of stars, the fasts, the feasts,
the thirsty deer,
the beautiful fields.

Also a rebel will, a burning lust
that shook him from God's way.
Only later, the abject penitence.
The grief of loss. The mourning.
The heart after God.

His humanity is thousands of years
away, but recognizable. In our anthems
we may yet make a dwelling for
the Most High, so was it not meet and right
for us to chant his words in our chancel
this Sunday morning?

GOD THE BEAR

Our God is a great bear
who leaves his pawprints
on the snowy trail of the lives
we are called to live, convincing us
that He was *here,* now He's moving
there. And though, as the sun
summits the high peaks, the graphics
of his purposes begin to thaw,
we've seen what we have seen.
The tracks invite us to step up
into the glisten of melt, over rocks
and rough scree. And though it is
out of sight, somewhere up there,
the summit raises its head with
such splendor that our blisters and bruises
are simply healed at the sight.

PILLARS OF THE CHURCH

Stonemasons, commissioned to
decorate the stony surfaces that uphold
the holy precincts (and maybe getting
bored with the standard beatified images
of cherubs sprouting rudimentary wings),
get creative, carving from imagination
acanthus leaves and vines coiling like
serpents. Scrolled corbels, acorns,
pomegranates, bunches of grapes cohabit
with fantastic beasts and lions and the graven
faces of saints and seraphim. Beings
maleficent and beneficent creep up
and down the stone pillars to proclaim
the generosity of all creation as it issues
from the mouth of God (and from mortal
imaginations dedicated to divine service).

"THE BOOK OF KELLS"

The calfskin page shows a full-page Gospel
opening with a glowing capital wound around with
serpents and sundry mythic bestiaries. Odd
human faces keep company with eldritch creatures
twined with vines, inhabited by dogs, eagles,
otters, serpents, open-jawed panthers. A cat sleeps,
lying along a transverse capital. All are tongued and
tamed by threes into mythical, mystical obedience
to ornament an iconography. Detailed with gold leaf
and the comely pigments of ground red lead, ocher,
green malachite and copper, circles within circles
coil about with knot-work like the intersecting roots of
sacred trees. All and everything in cumulates of three,
designed to call upon and praise the triune Godhead.

With what intent and joyful discipline, and with
what artful design and faith might we today
enact Good News for all created beings?
Look now. Look deep. With eyes and mind and heart
may we approach and join this realm of holy art.

PROPHECY

A shoot will come up from the stump of Jesse;
from his roots a branch will bear fruit.
—Isaiah 11:1

What is it
about the urgent
bud of green
poking from
this ancient tree's
rough stump
that reminds me of
the human improbability
of young Mary
giving birth?

MIDWINTER

The cold, penetrating, and
the wind. The church far.
On the way to worship
we lost our way and wondered,
How? Where? and found it on
a street corner where someone
had mounted a great tureen
of soup, steaming hot.

The loud weather, but *There!*
There! under the streetlamp
onions and potatoes voiced
their need to be consumed,
an aroma like the breath of God,
and the hungry people were fed,
and, strangers, we held hands in
a circle, giving thanks,
and worshiped.

"CLIMATE CHANGE KILLS ANTARCTIC MOSS"
—TIME *(October 8, 2018)*

You families of lichens,
your delicate abstractions of design
have for eons crept, obstinate,
across the faces of rocks—
unlikely flourishes urging for
survival at the harsh bottom
of the world.

You who have survived
extremes of wind and weather
speak now the language of loss
as waves wash their rising heat
over the stones that anchor you to
my planet. For all your tenacity,
you shrink now in a calamity
of our making.

I blame my own deficit on
the chill of age, while you
die as temperatures rise,
and I tell you that though
I would rather die of passion
than frigidity, I mourn
your shrinkage,
your demise.

You are so quiet.
Your only outcry is
loss until you
find yourself
almost not
there at all.

WINTER IN CHICAGO, 1960

Like the spreading roots of
a mighty oak, the heat-ducts of
our ancient basement furnace
would send, with a roar, a welcome
blast of hot air, like a psalm
of ascent, up two stories and through
our bedroom floor vents.
The children slept, unheeding,
warm under their covers.

Down below, steel wires bisected
the cellar space—strung horizons
holding up damp cloth diapers
to dry, like robes prepared for us
in some dank heaven, a gauze
yellowed again, again, by our
children's innocent incontinence.

And again, again, the gray wash water
got recycled through three loads of
laundry, like sin repented of and yet
returned to, like weekly confession
at St. Mary's down the block.

INUPIAT

—reflections on an image in National Geographic

Lying flat, head-down over
the ice floe's edge,
the hunter listens to the water,
straining to hear the profound
songs of whales.

His harpoon, beside him
on the ice, arrows forward, ready.
His ear finely tuned, heart
pounding with hunger and
desire, but patient as the great
ice shelf beneath him.

And the bowhead, somewhere
below, all ninety tons of him,
a deep hunter also,
strains krill through his thready
baleen, vocalizing—primal clicks,
grunts, sighs, soughs.

The man makes no sound. He cannot
speak whale. Yet from somewhere
deep in his own body of water
he invites leviathan
to meet him, meet his need.

Man and mammal, to be
joined in a feast of blood,
the dying in service to the living.

DOCTORING, BURMA

You wrote and told us how you hiked in,
you and the scouts stealing through secret
forest tracks, across rivers. How together
you cut bamboo enough to piece together
a house of healing, and a dwelling.
They began to arrive—the little families,
smelling of wood-smoke, burned out of
their villages by the military, plowed out of
their paddies. How to treat such injuries,
such loss? Someone came bearing a boy
whose one leg survived a landmine. Another,
a mother whose baby refused to be born.

In the simple clinic you treated fevers,
infections, open wounds, performed
surgeries on the bamboo floor, lit by flashlights.
During the monsoon the cold mountain streams
raged. You drew water for the rice pots,
the fish paste that became your daily diet.
In your classes the students learned anatomy
from a pig, to be roasted, later, for a Sunday feast.

The children loved their singing, and playing
in the sun with the chickens and puppies.
You sent your photos of them, the smiling
Karen, wearing their colorful hand-woven
clothing. Under the banana-leaf roof you slept
in a hammock, safe from snakes.

When you got home, you told us the stories
behind the stories. Then you went back again
for more healing, more stories, your own life
a narrative that holds us all in love and hope.

IMMIGRANT

When you are very young
there is no way you can see
ahead, plan your life. It may come
in spasms of rebuff and abuse.
And despair.

As it comes to the station,
the bus sighs, stops with a jerk
and a hiss before releasing its lone
passenger, who has traveled north to
this, what she hopes is the final stop.

Life happens, happens, happens.
She shows me the bruises.

She who has left behind conflict
and poverty and turmoil. Who imagines
what freedom might be like.

In fragments and spasms she
tells me her story. All she wants
is to draw a new life-line
clean as a plane's thread in the sky,
to live a new narrative,
to have children who'll tell their own
stories and be free
to dream their own dreams.

Who wonders if I can point
the way.

GALLERY

My husband
paints landscapes in acrylics
and every week or so
another rectangle of mountains
or forest, or ocean (from our
walk at the waterfront yesterday afternoon)
or the postcard someone sent
from their vacation moves
from his imagination onto canvas.
The images climb our walls
and gaze at us in the dining room,
commanding our attention,

I make suggestions: Add gray
to tone down the bright blue?
Lovely clouds, though.

The watercolors are
a different story. A lighter touch.
Pigment mediated by a wet brush,
for an unpredictable result as
the mystery of a color-wash seeps
across paper, damp, ungovernable,
images charming in their fluidity,
their fresh interpretation of the world.

DRIVING THE CASCADES

This highway through
the mountains,
this overwhelm,
this magnificence of
great, dead rocks, holds
its small miracles.

From my car, like an
insect on a window,
I consider this most
unwelcoming of settings
and there, right there—
life has kindled
an improbable green.

In some other century
a seed fell from its
mother-cone down
a precipitous cliff and
—*mirabile dictu*—
found a crack in
the rockface.

Like a toenail
that catches and holds,
a thin rootling thrust
into the blind cranny
its act of faith.

A hundred years,
and through today's
windshield
I glimpse the grown pine
and give thanks for
survival, mine,
and everyone else's,
planned before
the foundation
of the world.

LEAVING

Be like a tree and let the dead leaves drop.
—RUMI

The maple, on this wild
October day, lists each leaf
as it leaves. Each one,
perfectly formed in spring
like a green, newborn baby,
is now an old man,
a wrinkled woman.
To say *fall* is to tell truth.

PROMISES

We swallow words as the earth
swallows seeds. Sometimes indigestible,
ending in dry stubble. Maybe we sow
a single word of promise, with the dream
that something vital and fruited will rise
from the page as from a fecund field.
Like Aaron's staff that budded,
even a dry stick may thrust green shoots
from its stem, sprouts of expectation.

As now, as the rhythms of our speech vibrate
between us across the air, a soul music,
a kind of history is being made.
God's presence shimmering in every syllable.
On our pages, in our words, his gifts are
being given, and given, and given again.
Ours is a gospel promised to be true.

WHAT TO LISTEN FOR

What to listen for when
seeing is blotted out?

Say the fog has drifted in
from the Atlantic, crawling its
cold fingers up the rocks.

A tide of sound washing in
and out, indeterminate.

We've been there before
so we think we can fill in
the details. But of course, it
will never be the same.

Thanks be to God for all that
we cannot see. Yet.

ACKNOWLEDGMENTS

Christian Century
"Unable to See Far"
"Night Rainfall"
"Leaving"
"The Plane Trees"

Cresset
"Eve"

Crux
"The Book of Kells"
(first published as "Kells")
"Psalmody"
"Senior Citizen"
"Worship"

Englewood Review
"Eve"
"Grass"
"The 'O' in Hope"

McMaster Journal of Theology
"The Morning, Walking"
"Plunge"
"Vessel"

Pinyon Review
"Rhythms"
"Incoming Tides"
"Stream of Consciousness"
"Landscape"

Plough
"Cloth and Cup"

Valley Voices
"Presence"
"The 'O' in Hope"

Whale Road Review
"The Continent of Night"
"Driving to Willapa"
"The Knitting"

Windhover
"What My Bones Tell Me"

ABOUT PARACLETE PRESS

WHO WE ARE

As the publishing arm of the Community of Jesus, Paraclete Press presents a full expression of Christian belief and practice—from Catholic to Evangelical, from Protestant to Orthodox, reflecting the ecumenical charism of the Community and its dedication to sacred music, the fine arts, and the written word. We publish books, recordings, sheet music, and video/DVDs that nourish the vibrant life of the church and its people.

WHAT WE ARE DOING

BOOKS | PARACLETE PRESS BOOKS show the richness and depth of what it means to be Christian. While Benedictine spirituality is at the heart of who we are and all that we do, our books reflect the Christian experience across many cultures, time periods, and houses of worship.

We have many series, including *Paraclete Essentials*; *Paraclete Fiction*; *Paraclete Poetry*; *Paraclete Giants*; and for children and adults, *All God's Creatures*, books about animals and faith; and *San Damiano Books*, focusing on Franciscan spirituality. Others include *Voices from the Monastery* (men and women monastics writing about living a spiritual life today), *Active Prayer*, and new for young readers: *The Pope's Cat*. We also specialize in gift books for children on the occasions of Baptism and First Communion, as well as other important times in a child's life, and books that bring creativity and liveliness to any adult spiritual life.

The MOUNT TABOR BOOKS series focuses on the arts and literature as well as liturgical worship and spirituality; it was created in conjunction with the Mount Tabor Ecumenical Centre for Art and Spirituality in Barga, Italy.

MUSIC | The PARACLETE RECORDINGS label represents the internationally acclaimed choir *Gloriæ Dei Cantores*, the *Gloriæ Dei Cantores Schola*, and the other instrumental artists of the *Arts Empowering Life Foundation*.

Paraclete Press is the exclusive North American distributor for the Gregorian chant recordings from St. Peter's Abbey in Solesmes, France. Paraclete also carries all of the Solesmes chant publications for Mass and the Divine Office, as well as their academic research publications.

In addition, PARACLETE PRESS SHEET MUSIC publishes the work of today's finest composers of sacred choral music, annually reviewing over 1,000 works and releasing between 40 and 60 works for both choir and organ.

VIDEO | Our video/DVDs offer spiritual help, healing, and biblical guidance for a broad range of life issues including grief and loss, marriage, forgiveness, facing death, understanding suicide, bullying, addictions, Alzheimer's, and Christian formation.

Learn more about us at our website:
www.paracletepress.com
or phone us toll-free at 1.800.451.5006

SCAN
TO
READ

You may also be interested in...

Eye of the Beholder
Luci Shaw

ISBN 978-1-64060-085-0 | $18 | Trade paperback

The author of more than 35 collections of poetry and creative nonfiction over the last five decades, Luci Shaw describes her dedication to this art as a burden to "speak into a culture that finds it hard to listen."

The joy and responsibility of the poet is to focus on particulars within the universe, finding fragments of meaning that speak to the imagination. Ordinary things may reveal the extraordinary for those willing to take time to investigate and ponder. In this fresh collection of poems, Luci Shaw practices the art of seeing, and then writing what she sees, realizing that beauty is often focused in the *Eye of the Beholder*.

Eye of the Beholder is meant to awaken in readers awareness of the extraordinary in the ordinary. They will find in this collection a focus for meditation and be excited into their own imaginative writing.

———

"Luci Shaw crafts her poems in the way that she sees God's creation is crafted—seamlessly and with enviable freshness. Always honest with herself and her readers, she writes movingly about poetry and prayer and growing older. She has written some of the best recent poems I have read about aging. Aging itself may not be marvelous, but Luci Shaw's are marvelous poems. It is always a pleasure to spend time with her work."—**Mark Jarman**, author of *The Heronry*

Available at bookstores
Paraclete Press | 1-800-451-5006 | www.paracletepress.com

CPSIA information can be obtained
at www.ICGtesting.com
Printed in the USA
BVHW030918040521
606354BV00002B/294

9 781640 605145